THE
RUBAIYAT
OF A
PERSIAN
KITTEN

THE
RUBAIYAT
OF A
PERSIAN
KITTEN

BY
OLIVER HERFORD

RIZZOLI
NEW YORK

Published in the United States of America in 1993 by
Rizzoli International Publications, Inc.
300 Park Avenue South, New York, New York 10010

Library of Congress Cataloging-in-Publication Data

Herford, Oliver, 1863–1935.
    The Rubaiyat of a Persian kitten / Oliver Herford.
        p.   cm
    ISBN 0-8478-1707-5
    1. Cats—Poetry.   I. Title.
PS3515.E62R8   1993
811'.52—dc20   92-38393
                                                   CIP

Editor: Lois Brown

Design by David Larkin

Printed and bound in Singapore

THE
RUBAIYAT
OF A
PERSIAN
KITTEN

Wake! for the Golden Cat has
              put to flight
The Mouse of Darkness
              with his Paw of Light:
Which means, in Plain and
                   simple every-day
Unoriental Speech—The Dawn
                        is bright.

They say the Early Bird the
　　　Worm shall taste.
Then rise, O Kitten! Wherefore,
　　　　　sleeping, waste
　　The fruits of Virtue? Quick!
　　　　　　the Early Bird
Will soon be on the Flutter—O
　　　　　make haste!

The Early Bird has gone, and
with him ta'en
The Early Worm—Alas! the
Moral's plain,
O Senseless Worm! Thus,
thus we are repaid
For Early Rising—I shall doze
again.

The Mouse makes merry 'mid
    the Larder Shelves,
The Bird for Dinner in the
      Garden delves.
  I often wonder what the
       creatures eat
One half so toothsome as they
     are Themselves.

And that Inverted Bowl of
       Skyblue Delf
That helpless lies upon the
           Pantry Shelf—
    Lift not your eyes to It for
             help, for It
Is quite as empty as you are
          yourself.

The Ball no question makes of
  Ayes of Noes,
But right or left, as strikes the
            Kitten, goes;
  Yet why, altho' I toss it Far
            Afield,
It still returneth—Goodness
            only knows!

O Secret Presence that my
　　likeness feigns,
And yet, quicksilver-like, eludes
　　　　my pains—
　　In vain I look for Him
　　　　behind the glass;
He is not there, and yet He still
　　　　remains.

What out of airy Nothing to

      invoke

A senseless Something to resist

           the stroke

    Of unpermitted Paw—upon

            the pain

Of Everlasting Penalties—if

          broke.

) sometimes think the Pussy-
            Willows grey
Are Angel Kittens who have lost
                        their way,
    And every Bulrush on the
                        river bank
A Cat-Tail from some lovely
                        Cat astray.

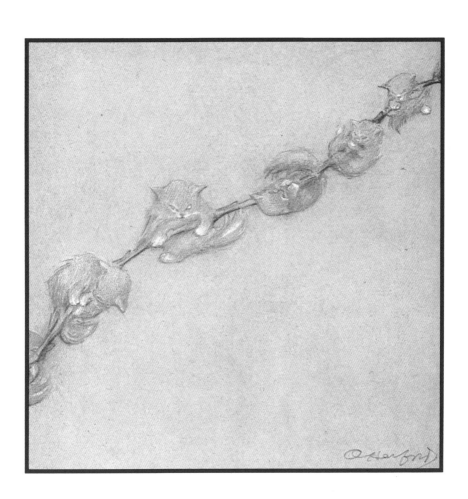

Sometimes I think perchance
        that Allah may,
When he created Cats, have
                    thrown away
    The Tails He marred in
            making, and they grew
To Cat-Tails and to Pussy-
                Willows grey.

And lately, when I was not
Feeling Fit,
Bereft alike of Piety and Wit,
There came an Angel Shape
and offered me
A Fragrant Plant and bid me
taste of it.

'Twas that reviving Herb,
    that Spicy Weed,
The Cat-Nip. Tho' 'tis good in
                time of need,
    Ah, feed upon it lightly, for
                who knows
To what unlovely antics it may
                lead.

Strange—is it not?—that of
the numbers who
Before me passed this Door of
Darkness thro',
Not one returns thro' it again,
altho'
Ofttimes I've waited here an
hour or two.

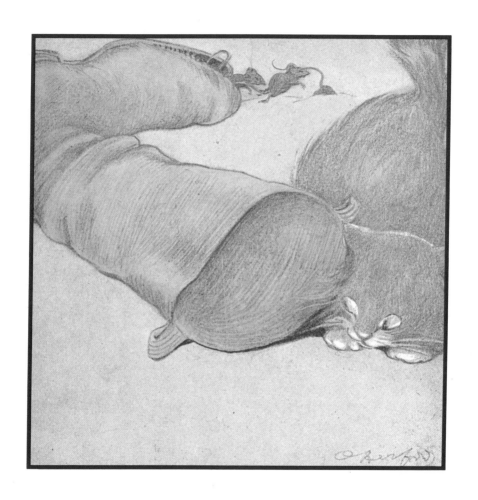

'Tis but a Tent where takes
his one Night's Rest
A Rodent to the Realms of
Death address'd,
When Cook, arising, looks for
him and then—
Baits, and prepares it for
another Guest.

They say the Lion and the
       Lizard keep
The Courts where Jamshýd
        gloried and drank deep.
  The Lion is my cousin; I
            don't know
Who Jamshýd is—nor shall it
         break my sleep.

)mpotent glimpses of the
Game displayed
Upon the Counter—temptingly
arrayed;
Hither and thither moved or
checked or weighed,
And one by one back in the Ice
Chest laid.

What if the Sole could fling
        the Ice aside,
And with me to some Area's
                haven glide—
    Were't not a Shame, were't
                not a shame for it
In this Cold Prison crippled to
                abide?

Some for the Glories of the
 Sole, and Some
Mew for the proper Bowl of
 Milk to come.
 Ah, take the Fish and let your
 Credit go,
And plead the rumble of an
 empty Tum.

One thing is certain: tho' this
    Stolen Bite
Should be my last and Wrath
        consume me quite,
  One taste of It within the Area
          caught
Better than at the Table lost
        outright.

)ndeed, indeed Repentance oft
before
I swore, but was I hungry when
I swore?
And then and then came Cook
—with Hose in hand—
And drowned my glory in a
sorry pour.

What without asking hither
harried whence,
And without asking whither
harried hence—
O, many a taste of that
forbidden Sole
Must down the memory of that
Insolence.

Heaven, but the vision of a
Flowing Bowl;
And Hell, the sizzle of a Frying
Sole
Heard in the hungry Darkness,
where Myself,
So rudely cast, must impotently
roll.

The Vine has a tough Fibre

which about

While clings by Being;—let the

Canine Flout

Till his Bass Voice be pitched

to such loud key

It shall unlock the door I mew

without.

Up from the Basement to the
        Seventh Flat
I rose, and on the Crown of
                Fashion sat,
    And many a Ball unravelled
            by the way—
But not the Master's angry Bawl
            of "Scat!"

*T*hen to the Well of Wisdom I
—and lo!
With my own Paw I wrought to
Make it flow,
And This was all the Harvest
that I reaped:
We come like Kittens and like
Cats we go.

Why be this Ink the fount of
                Wit?—who dare
Blaspheme the glistening Pen-
                        drink as a snare?
A Blessing?—I should spread
                        it, should I not?
And if a Curse—why, then upset
                        it!—there!

A moment's Halt, a
        momentary Taste
Of Bitter, and amid the Trickling
                        Waste
    I wrought strange shapes from
                Máh to Máhi, yet
I know not what I wrote, nor
                why they chased.

Now I beyond the Pale am
		safely past.
O, but the long, long time their
				Rage shall last,
Which, tho' they call to supper,
				I shall heed
As a Stone Cat should heed a
				Pebble cast.

And that perverted Soul
      beneath the Sky
They call the Dog—Heed not his
             angry Cry;
   Not all his Threats can make
         me budge one bit,
Nor all his Empty Bluster
              terrify.

They are no other than a
      moving Show
of whirling Shadow Shapes that
               come and go
      Me-ward thro' Moon illumined
          Darkness hurled,
In midnight, by the Lodgers in
         the Row.

Myself when young did eagerly
frequent
The Backyard Fence and heard
great Argument
About it, and About, yet
evermore
Came out with Fewer Fur than in
I went.

Ah, me! if you and I could

　　　but conspire

To grasp this Sorry Scheme of

　　　　　things entire,

　　Would we not shatter it to

　　　　　bits, and then

Enfold it nearer to our Heart's

　　　　　Desire?

Tho' Two and Two make Four

     by rule of line,

Or they make Twenty-two by

         Logic fine,

   Of all the Figures one may

         fathom, I

Shall ne'er be floored by anything

         but Nine.

And fear not lest Existence
shut the Door
On You and Me, to open it no
more.
The Cream of Life from out
your Bowl shall pour
Nine times—ere it lie broken on
the Floor.

So, if the Fish you Steal—the
Cream you drink—
Ends in what all begins and ends
in, Think,
Unless the Stern Recorder
points to Nine,
Tho' They would drown you—
still you shall not sink.

Editor's note on *The Rubáiyát of Omar Khayyám*

In the eleventh century when Omar Khayyám wrote the quatrains known as *The Rubáiyát of Omar Khayyám*, he was a celebrated mathematician and astronomer to Sultan Malek Shah. He was not considered a poet, and little did he know that his verse would live for centuries, eventually becoming the most popular book of poetry ever to appear in the English language. You may not know of Omar, but you probably have heard:

> 'Tis all a Chequer-board of Nights and Days
> Where Destiny with Men for Pieces plays:
> Hither and Thither moves, and mates, and slays,
> And one by one back in the Closet lays.

Born in Naishápúr, Persia, about 1048, Omar took the name Khayyám ("the tentmaker") from his father's trade. He wrote an authoritative book on algebra, revised the calendar, and was generally known as a lover of truth and beauty and a freethinker who detested bigots and narrow minds.

WAKE! for Morning in the Bowl of Night
Has flung the Stone that puts the Stars to Flight:
    And Lo! the Hunter of the East has caught
The Sultan's Turret in a Noose of Light.

In the eighteenth century Edward FitzGerald (1809–1883), a Briton who had never been to Persia and wasn't even a scholar of the Oriental world, discovered the old quatrains and translated them. He did not attempt to produce close, literal translations, but freely paraphrased the quatrains, producing an English version that today is considered a masterpiece of English verse.

The poetry of *The Rubáiyát* is full of desire, regret, and the knowledge that:

The Moving Finger writes; and, having writ,
Moves on: nor all thy Piety nor Wit
    Shall lure it back to cancel half a Line,
Nor all thy Tears wash out a Word of it.

Omar expresses skepticism and doubt about life and religion and man's ability to arrive at certainty; his poems are filled with a sense of being disregarded by fortune:

> Ah Love! could thou and I with Fate conspire
> To grasp this sorry Scheme of Things entire,
>   Would not we shatter it to bits—and then
> Remould it nearer to the Heart's Desire!

His advice is to make the most of this world; to sooth the soul through the senses and to accept life as it is without speculating why and what might be:

> Come, fill the Cup, and in the Fire of Spring
> The Winter Garment of Repentance fling:
>   The Bird of Time has but a little way
> To Fly—and Lo! the Bird is on the Wing.

With them the Seed of Wisdom did I sow,
And with my own hand labor'd it to grow:
    And this was all the Harvest that I reap'd—
"I came like Water, and like Wind I go."

Enter Oliver Herford (1863–1935) in 1904, an English humorist and writer of children's literature, who, with a wink at Omar's fatalism wrote his own *Rubáiyát* with the main character a Persian kitten who goes in search of a sip of milk and encounters outrageous fortune. But there's a twist to this story, as kitty, with nine lives, triumphs in the end. As for Omar,

Ah, Moon of my Delight who know'st no wane;
The Moon of Heav'n is rising once again:
    How oft hereafter rising shall she look
Through this same Garden after me—in vain!